99 Tricks an

Microsoft® Office Project

Including Microsoft® Project

2000 to 2007

The Casual User's "Survival Guide"

By

Paul E Harris

of

Eastwood Harris Pty Ltd

99 TRICKS & TRAPS for Microsoft Office Project

DISCLAIMER

AUTHOR AND PUBLISHER

Paul E Harris
Eastwood Harris Pty Ltd
PO Box 4032
Doncaster Heights 3109
Victoria
Australia
harrispe@eh.com.au
http://www.eh.com.au
Tel: +61 (0)4 1118 7701
Fax: +61 (0)3 9846 7700

Please send any comments on this publication to the author.

ISBN 978-1-921059-19-3

24 May 2007

99 TRICKS & TRAPS for Microsoft Office Project

CURRENT BOOKS PUBLISHED BY EASTWOOD HARRIS

Planning and Scheduling Using Microsoft Office Project 2007
Including Microsoft Project 2000 to 2003, published March 2007
ISBN 978-1-921059-15-5 - B5 Paperback, ISBN 978-1-921059-16-2 - A4 Spiral

PRINCE2 Planning & Control Using Microsoft Project
Updated for Microsoft Office Project 2007, published March 2007
ISBN978-1-921059-17-9 - B5 Paperback

Planning and Control Using Microsoft Project and PMBOK® Guide Third Edition -
Updated for Microsoft Office Project 2007, published March 2007
ISBN 978-1-921059-18-6 - B5 Paperback

Planning Using Primavera® Project Planner P3® Version 3.1 Revised 2006,
published March 2000
ISBN 1-921059-13-3 Spiral Bound

Planning Using Primavera® SureTrak Project Manager Version 3.0 Revised 2006,
ISBN 1-921059-14-1 A4 Spiral Bound, published June 2000

Project Planning and Scheduling Using Primavera® Contractor Version 4.1
for the Construction Industry, published January 2005
ISBN 1-921059-04-4 A4 Paperback, ISBN 1-921059-05-2 A4 Spiral Bound

Planning and Scheduling Using Primavera® Version 5.0 for E&C,
published December 2005
ISBN 1-921059-09-5 A4 Paperback, ISBN 1-921059-10-9 A4 Spiral Bound

Planning and Scheduling Using Primavera® Version 5.0 for IT Project Office,
published December 2005
ISBN 1-921059-11-7 A4 Paperback, ISBN 1-921059-12-5 A4 Spiral Bound

SUPERSEDED BOOKS BY THE AUTHOR

Planning and Scheduling Using Microsoft® Project 2000
Planning and Scheduling Using Microsoft® Project 2002
Planning and Scheduling Using Microsoft® Project 2003
Project Planning and Scheduling Using Primavera Enterprise - Team Play
Project Planning and Scheduling Using Primavera Enterprise - P3e & P3e/c
Project Planning and Scheduling Using Primavera® Version 4.1
for IT Project Office
Project Planning and Scheduling Using Primavera® Version 4.1 for E&C
Planning Using Primavera Project Planner P3 Version 2.0
Planning Using Primavera Project Planner P3 Version 3.0
Project Planning Using SureTrak for Windows Version 2.0

SERVICES OFFERED BY EASTWOOD HARRIS PTY LTD

Eastwood Harris specializes in setting up and running project controls systems with a focus on Primavera Systems and Microsoft Project software; we offer the following services:

Project Planning and Scheduling Training Courses using Primavera Enterprise, Contractor, P3, SureTrak or Microsoft Office Project

➢ Eastwood Harris offers one-to-one training to get your new schedulers up and running quickly, without the delay of waiting for the next course and at the same time building up your own project schedule.

➢ We also run in-house training courses on any of these software packages. This is a very cost efficient method of training your personnel.

➢ We are able to assist you in setting up a scheduling environment. This includes designing coding structures, writing procedures, training and other implementation processes.

➢ Eastwood Harris can write specialized training material that will incorporate your organization's methodology into the Eastwood Harris training manuals and develop student workshops tailored to your requirements. Project personnel will be able to use these books as reference books after the course.

Selection and Implementation of Project Management Systems

➢ Eastwood Harris will assist you by conducting an internal review of your requirements and match this requirement analysis against the functionality of packaged software.

➢ We are then able to assist you in the implementation of these systems, including writing policies and procedures and training personnel, to ensure a smooth transition to your new system.

Dispute Resolution

➢ Eastwood Harris is able to analyze your subcontractor's schedules in the event of claims and provide you with a clear picture of the schedule in relation to the claim.

Schedule Conversion

➢ Eastwood Harris is able to convert your schedules from one software package to another. The conversion of schedules is often time consuming, so let us do it for you.

Please contact the author for more information on these services.

99 TRICKS & TRAPS for Microsoft Office Project

TABLE OF CONTENTS

© *Eastwood Harris*

1 IMPORTANT THINGS

Readers of this book should be familiar with:

❖ The basic functions of Microsoft Project and

❖ The theory of Critical Path including Early dates, Late dates and Float calculations. Microsoft Project uses Slack for term Float.

Microsoft Project has functions that catch out users. You should understand these functions and be able to identify when they have been used inadvertently.

1.1 The "Delete" Key

Striking the delete key will delete data without warning. So keep your fingers away from it. I usually place the Tasks ID in the description of the last task so I know if I have deleted a task in error.

1.2 Typing a Date or Dragging a Task Sets a Constraint!

Functions that set a task constraint without warning::

❖ Typing or selecting a start date in a **Start** date field will set a **Start No Earlier Than** constraint

❖ Typing or selecting a finish date in a **Finish** date field will set a **Finish No Earlier Than** constraint

❖ Dragging a bar in the Gantt Chart View will set a **Start No Earlier Than** constraint

Note: You need to be very careful when dragging tasks or typing into date fields as this will set a constraint and the tasks will not move forward in time when predecessors are removed.

1.3 *Indicators Column*

The **Indicators** column is a very useful feature that specifies when a task has an attribute that is different from a normal task created by inserting a new task. The indicators column will display a constraint icon when a constraint has been set:

❖ Before entering a date in a Start or Finish field or Dragging a Task, the indicator column is blank:

❖ After entering a date in a Start or Finish field or Dragging a Task, a constraint is set. There now is a Constraint indicator in the Indicator column:

❖ A note displays when the indicator field has the mouse pointer placed over the indicator cell:

❖ The indicator column shows a different icon when tasks have Notes, Task Calendar or a Constraint conflict causing Negative Float (Slack):

		Task Name	Dur	Start	Finish
		Task with a note	5 d	3 May	7 May
8		Task with a constraint	5 d	6 May	12 May
		Task with constraint conflict	2 d	3 May	4 May

Note: No indicator is displayed with a Deadline Date, unless Negative Float is created.

1.4 Why Are Tasks Scheduled before the Predecessors?

There are a couple of reasons why tasks would be displayed before a predecessor relationship would allow them to be scheduled:

❖ An **Actual Start** date has been set, or

❖ **Tasks will always honor their constraint dates** is set and a task has been assigned Late constraint.

1.4.1 Actual Start Date

You may have assigned an Actual Start to a task by entering a date in the Actual Start field or entering a % Complete.

❖ Once an Actual Start Date has been set a predecessor relationship does not affect the Actual Start date.

❖ A predecessor relationship may cause an in-progress Task with an Actual Start date to split when the **Tools**, **Options...**, **Schedule** tab **Split in progress tasks** option has been checked.

1.4.2 Tasks Will Always Honor Their Constraint Dates

There is an option in the **Tools**, **Options...**, **Schedule** form titled **Tasks will always honor their constraint dates**. This option allows a task to be scheduled before the predecessors when the successor has a **Finish no later than** or **Start no later than** constraint. In effect, this option will make all constraints override relationships.

For example, a task with a **Must Start On** constraint, which is prior to a predecessor's Finish Date, will display an Early Start on the constraint date and not the scheduled date. The **Total Slack** may not calculate as the difference between Late Start and Early Start. Examine the following two examples with the option box checked and unchecked:

❖ Tasks will always honor their constraint dates: option box checked:

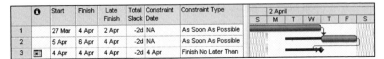

Task 3 starts before the predecessor finishes and the total slack of the second task is calculated as -2 days, which is not the difference between the Early Finish and the Late Finish. This constraint does not adhere to commonly accepted Total Float calculations.

❖ **Tasks will always honor their constraint dates**: option box NOT checked and the Total Float is calculated correctly:

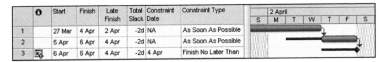

It is suggested that this option is <u>NEVER</u> switched on, as the schedule may appear to be achievable when it is not.

1.5   The Logic Keeps Changing!

The logic will change if a task is dragged to another position when **Autolink inserted or moved tasks** option is turned on.

This option is intended to be used to automatically link new inserted tasks with a predecessor to the task above and a successor to the task below.

The downside of this function is that when the task is moved this function will change the existing predecessors and successors of the:

❖ Moved task,

❖ Original tasks that were above and below the moved task, and

❖ New tasks that are now above and below the moved tasks.

This function will potentially make substantial changes to your project logic and may affect the overall project duration. It is suggested that this option is **NEVER** switched on, as dragging an activity to a new location may completely change the logic of a schedule without warning.

Select **Tools**, **Options...**, **Schedule** tab and uncheck **Autolink inserted or moved tasks**.

1.6   The Project Will Not Open!

Microsoft Project 2007 has a new file format that may not be opened with Microsoft Project 2000-2003. Microsoft Project 2000-2003 format may be saved from Microsoft Project 2007.

An example of this process is shown below:

❖ Original Logic:

	Task Name	Duration	Predec- essors	Succ- essors	Apr '07					
					12	19	26	2	9	16
1	A	5 days		2						
2	B	5 days	1	3						
3	C	5 days	2	4						
4	D	5 days	3	5						
5	E	5 days	4							

❖ Task D dragged with **Autolink inserted or moved tasks** checked. Note the logic has changed on many tasks:

	Task Name	Duration	Predec- essors	Succ- essors	Apr '07					
					12	19	26	2	9	16
1	A	5 days		2						
2	D	5 days	1	3						
3	B	5 days	2	4						
4	C	5 days	3	5						
5	E	5 days	4							

❖ Task D dragged with **Autolink inserted or moved tasks** unchecked. The logic has not changed:

	Task Name	Duration	Predec- essors	Succ- essors	Apr '07					
					12	19	26	2	9	16
1	A	5 days		3						
2	D	5 days	4	5						
3	B	5 days	1	4						
4	C	5 days	3	2						
5	E	5 days	2							

1.7 Why Do New Tasks Have an Early Start Constraint?

Unlike other scheduling software, Microsoft Project normally ignores the Status Date when calculating a progressed schedule. It schedules tasks without an Actual Start or predecessors or constraints on the Project Start Date, or as close to the Project Start Date as calendars permit. It does not commence the incomplete portions of Tasks after the Status Date. The **Tools**, **Options...**, **Schedule** tab has a **New tasks:** option of either:

❖ **Start on Current Date**, or

❖ **Start on Project Start Date**.

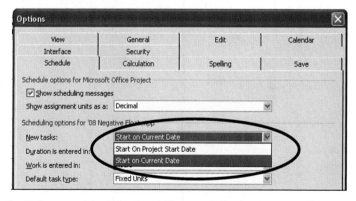

❖ When set to **Start on Current Date**, new tasks are created with an **Early Start Constraint** set to the **Current Date**.

❖ When set to **Start on Project Start Date**, new tasks are created without a constraint. When the **Autolink inserted or new tasks:** is switched off all new tasks will schedule on the Project Start Date.

1.8   Recommended Schedule Options

It is best to keep a schedule as simple as possible. I recommend that you consider the following Schedule Options as a good starting point if you have limited experience in scheduling software:

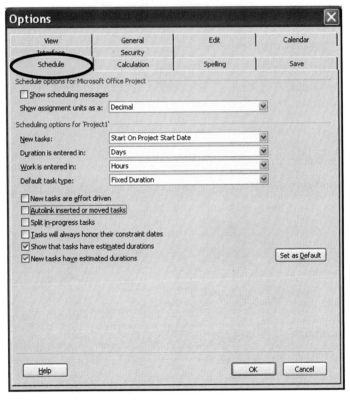

❖ The option of displaying a new task with a "?" after the duration is called an **Estimated Duration**. The default setting may be changed in the **Tools**, **Options...**, **Schedule** tab.

Note: Most of the other options are covered in this book.

2 CALENDAR SURVIVAL GUIDE

2.1 Role of the Project Calendar

The project calendar is assigned to a project in the **Project**, **Project Information...** form:

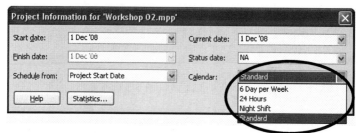

❖ New tasks are not assigned a calendar by default.

❖ All tasks that have not been assigned a Task Calendar calculate their Early Finish date from their Early Start date plus the Duration calculated over the Project Calendar.

❖ Therefore, a five-day duration task with a five-day workweek calendar, starting Wednesday, with Saturday and Sunday as non workdays, will finish at the end of the workday on the following Tuesday, see the picture below:

Note: A change to the Project Calendar may make substantial changes to the elapsed duration of all activities that have not been assigned a Task Calendar.

2.2 Guidelines for Creating Calendars

Calendars are created using the **Tools**, **Change Working Time...** form.

An unlimited number of calendars may be created:

❖ One calendar is assigned as the Project Calendar.

❖ Each task and resource may be assigned a unique calendar.

❖ The calendar assigned to a resource may be further edited to represent the resource's unique availability.

There are some guidelines that should be considered when contemplating the use of multiple calendars. These are summarized below:

❖ If you are able to schedule a project with only one calendar then do so; keep the schedule simple.

❖ The work hours per day for all calendars on a project should be the same for each workday, otherwise the Summary Durations in days will not all calculate correctly.

❖ Keep the Start and Finish times for all calendars the same, otherwise the Default Start and End Time will be incorrect for some tasks when Constraints or Actual Dates are assigned without times.

❖ When resources are assigned the resource calendar takes preference, unless **Scheduling ignores resource calendars** is checked in the **Task Information** form.

2.3 Display of Duration in Days

Microsoft Project effectively calculates in hours. The value of the duration in days is calculated using the parameter entered in the **Hours per day:** field in the **Tools**, **Options...**, **Calendar** tab. It is **VERY IMPORTANT** to understand that all duration in days are calculated using **ONLY** this parameter with **EVERY** calendar irrespective of the number of hours per day in any calendar.

For example, when the **Options** form **Hours per day:** value is set to "8" then tasks assigned:

❖ An 8-hours per day calendar will have durations in days displayed correctly, and

❖ An 24-hours per day calendar will have durations in days displayed incorrectly,

The picture below shows:

❖ Task 1 has the correct duration of 5 days, but

❖ Task 2 also shows a 5-day duration that is clearly misleading.

	Task Calendar	Duration	Mon 1	Tue 2	Wed 3	Thu 4	Fri 5
1	8 Hours per Day	5 days					
2	24 Hours per Day	5 days					

❖ Tasks 4 and 5 display the duration in hours and this is not misleading as the calendar column is also displayed.

	Task Calendar	Duration	Mon 1	Tue 2	Wed 3	Thu 4	Fri 5
4	8 Hours per Day	40 hrs					
5	24 Hours per Day	40 hrs					

It is **STRONGLY RECOMMENDED** that you avoid assigning calendars with a different number of hours per day wherever possible.

There are some workable options to ensure that the durations in days are calculated and/or displayed correctly:

❖ All the calendars used on a project schedule should have the same number of hours per day for each day. This value is entered in the **Hours per day:** field in the Options.

❖ When there is a requirement to use a different number of hours per day (in either the same calendar or in different calendars) then all durations should only be displayed in hours and the Task Calendar displayed. The **Duration is entered in:** field in the **Tools**, **Options...**, **Edit** tab should be set to **Hours**. Thus all durations will be entered by default in hours.

❖ A Customized Field may be used to calculate and display the correct duration using a formula. The formula below may be used to calculate the correct duration in a **Duration** field of tasks scheduled on a 24 hours per day calendar when the Project Calendar is an 8 hour per day calendar:

IIf([Task Calendar]="24 hr/day",[Duration]*0.33,[Duration])

2.4   *How to Assign Task Calendars*

A task may be assigned a calendar that is different from the Project Calendar by:

❖ Displaying the **Task Calendar** column and editing the Task Calendar from this column, or

❖ Opening the **Task Information** form **Advanced** tab by double-clicking on the task.

After a calendar has been assigned, an icon will appear in the **Indicators** column and the calendar name displayed in the Task Calendar column, as shown in the picture below for the **Installation Requirements** task:

	ⓘ	Task Name	Task Calendar
3		Technical Feasibility Study	None
4	🗐	Installation Requirements	6 Day Working Week
5		Component Bids	None

❖ The task Finish date, Total Float, Free Float and Variances from a Baseline will be calculated on the Task Calendar. This often leads to confusion for new users as tasks on a 24-hour/day calendar will have different Float than tasks on an 8-hour/day calendar.

❖ When resources are assigned to a Task the Finish date is calculated on the Resource calendar, unless the Task has been assigned a calendar and the box in the **Task Information** form **Advanced** tab **Scheduling ignores resource calendars** is checked. Then the task duration is calculated based on the assigned Task Calendar.

2.5   Other Things Task Calendars Affect

2.5.1   Float

Float (Slack) is calculated on the Task Calendar. Both tasks below have been scheduled to finish at 17:00 hours but have different Float values:

	Duration	Task Calendar	Total Slack	26 March				
				M	T	W	T	F
1	8 hrs	8 Hours/Day	16 hrs					
2	15 hrs	24 Hours/Day	42 hrs					

2.5.2   Lags

Lags are calculated on the **Successor Calendar**, and therefore affect the start date and time of successors:

Duration	Task Calendar	Predecessors	2 April					
			S	M	T	W	T	F
8 hrs	None							
8 hrs	None	1FS+16 hrs						
24 hrs	24 Hours	1FS+16 hrs						

Note: Microsoft Project 2000 uses the **Project Calendar** to calculate lags, therefore files may calculate differently in 2000 from later versions. The example below is the file from the picture above and opened in Microsoft Project 2000:

Duration	Task Calendar	Predecessors	2 April					
			S	M	T	W	T	F
8 hrs	None							
8 hrs	None	1FS+16 hrs						
24 hrs	24 Hours	1FS+16 hrs						

2.6 *Resource Calendars*

Each resource is created with its very own editable calendar. Here are some important points:

❖ Each new resource is assigned a copy of the current Project Calendar as its Base Calendar.

❖ This Resource Base Calendar may be changed in the **Resource Sheet** or **Change Working Time** form to another Base Calendar.

❖ Any change to a Base Calendar will be reflected in any Resource Calendar.

❖ The Resource Calendar may be edited to suit the availability of the resource. Days may be made non workdays to represent holidays, etc.

❖ Normally the duration of a resourced task calculated from the Resource Calendar.

❖ When there are two or more resources assigned to a task and they have different end dates due to different calendars or assignments, then the task will finish at the end of the longest resource.

❖ When a Task has been assigned a calendar and the check box in the **Task Information** form **Advanced** tab **Scheduling ignores resource calendars** is checked the task duration is then calculated from the Task calendar.

❖ The Finish date may be calculated differently after a task is assigned one or more resources when the Resources Calendars are not the same as the Task Calendar.

2.7   Which Calendar is the Task Using?

When it is difficult to understand which calendar is being used for calculating the Finish Date, try the checklist below:

❖ Check the Project Calendar in the **Project**, **Project Information...** form, the default for new tasks,

❖ Then check the Task Calendar in the **Task** form **Advanced** tab or a Task Calendar column,

❖ Next check if resources are assigned to the task,

❖ Finally check the Resource Calendar for holidays.

The rules are as follows:

❖ When NO Task Calendar and NO resources assigned, then the Project Calendar is used.

❖ When a Task Calendar is assigned and there are NO resources assigned then the Task Calendar is being used.

❖ When there are Resources assigned and the **Scheduling ignores resource calendars** is checked, then the Task Calendar is used, or the Project Calendar when there is no Task calendar is set.

❖ With Resources assigned and the **Scheduling ignores resource calendars** is NOT checked, then the Resource Calendar is being used.

A common mistake is assigning a task an edited task calendar, then at a later date assigning resources without editing the resource calendars to match the task calendars and not realizing that the task durations no longer calculate the same.

2.8   Default Start and End Time

You may notice tasks span one day longer in the bar chart than their duration. This often occurs when the calendar start and finish times are edited but the **Default start time:** and **Default end time:** are not adjusted to match the task calendars.

These times **MUST** be aligned to the Project Calendar when:

❖ Constraints are assigned to tasks, and

❖ Actual Start or Actual Finish Dates are assigned.

When these times are not aligned then tasks may be displayed one day longer than their assigned duration. The picture below shows a 3-day task spanning four days because the Calendar start time is 8:00 am and the Default start time is 9:00 am.

Duration	Start	Finish	Tuesday	Wednesday	Thursday	Friday
3 days	Tue 9:00 AM	Fri 9:00 AM				

❖ The software assigns a **Default start time:** and **Default end time:** when a date is entered in a field but a time is not entered.

These times are set in the **Options..., Calendar** tab which may be accessed by:

❖ Clicking the Options... button from the **Tools, Change working time...** form, or

❖ Selecting the **Tools, Options..., Calendar** tab.

When a schedule has calendars with different start or finish times then to assist the reading and interpretation of the schedule:

❖ The Task Calendar should be displayed in columns, and

❖ The time should be displayed with the date in start and finish columns by selecting **Tools**, **Options**..., **View** tab and selecting an appropriate date format.

2.9 Finish Variance Calculation

❖ The Finish Variance is the difference between the Early Finish and Baseline Finish.

❖ Variances are calculated on the Task Calendar.

The picture below shows two milestones that have their Baselines set and have been delayed one week:

Task Calendar	Finish Variance	26 March							2 April	
		M	T	W	T	F	S	S	M	T
5 days per week	5 days	◇							◆	
7 days per week	7 days	◇							◆	

❖ The milestone on a 5-day per week calendar has a 5-day variance which is not the elapsed variance, and

❖ The milestone on a 7-day per week calendar has a 7-day variance which is the elapsed variance.

Note: When you need to calculate a milestone variance in calendar days, it is best to place the milestone on a 7-day per week calendar without holidays to ensure the Variance calculates the elapsed duration.

3 TRICKY STUFF

3.1 Task Splitting

3.1.1 What is Splitting?

Splitting a task puts a break in a Task, leaving:

❖ The Duration value unchanged but the elapsed duration increased, and

❖ Resources assigned to a split task are not assigned work during the splits:

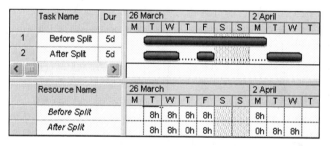

	Task Name	Dur	26 March							2 April			
			M	T	W	T	F	S	S	M	T	W	T
1	Before Split	5d											
2	After Split	5d											

Resource Name	26 March							2 April			
	M	T	W	T	F	S	S	M	T	W	T
Before Split		8h	8h	8h	8h			8h			
After Split		8h	8h	0h	8h			0h	8h	8h	

3.1.2 Splitting a Task Manually

To split a task manually: right-click on the [⊞] **Split Task** button on the **Formatting** toolbar; then click on the point on the Gantt Chart bar where the split is to be made; then right-click. A **Split Tasks:** box will appear. Drag the task to split it:

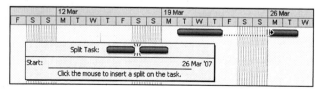

	12 Mar							19 Mar							26 Mar		
F	S	S	M	T	W	T	F	S	S	M	T	W	T	F	S	S	M	T	W

Split Task:
Start: 26 Mar '07
Click the mouse to insert a split on the task.

The finish and start dates and times of each split are not available through the user interface.

3.1.3   Splitting In-progress Tasks

When the **Split in-progress tasks** option is enabled in the **Tools**, **Options...**, **Schedule** form, a task will **Split** automatically when a task commences before its predecessor finishes.

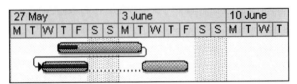

Microsoft Project is inconsistent when the **Split in-progress tasks** option is used with tasks that are assigned with one of the following options:

❖ An Actual Start and 0% Complete — these tasks are not split, or

❖ An Actual Start and % Complete set between 1% and 99% Complete — these tasks are split.

The two examples below are from the same schedule, both with the **Split in-progress tasks** option checked, one with 0% and one with 1%. You will notice the task assigned 0% has an earlier Finish Date than the task assigned 1% Complete, which has split.

You therefore need to pay careful attention to any warning messages Microsoft Project presents.

3.1.4   Hiding a Bar Split

Even though the task has been split, bar splits may be hidden. Select **Format**, **Layout...** to open the **Layout** form and uncheck the **Show bar splits**.

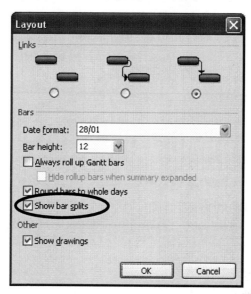

❖ The 10-day activity below has a split with an elapsed duration of 17 days:

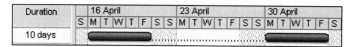

❖ The 10-day activity below has a hidden split and an elapsed duration of 17 days, which may be misleading:

3.1.5   Removing a Bar Split

A split is removed by:

❖ Dragging the split part back with the mouse.

❖ Turning off **Split in-progress tasks** in the **Tools**, **Options...**, **Schedule** form.

Note: Sometimes a tail of dots is left after the split has been removed. This tail also has to be dragged back to the end of the task and often the duration reset for the task to calculate correctly.

3.2   *Deadline Date*

Microsoft Project does not allow setting two task constraints except in the case of a **Deadline Date**.

❖ A Deadline Date is set in the **Task Information** form **Advanced** tab or in the Deadline Date column.

❖ **Deadline Date** allows the setting of a date by which a task should be completed.

❖ A **Deadline Date** is similar to placing a **Finish No Later Than** constraint and affects the calculation of the **Late Finish** date and float of the activity.

❖ A constraint such as an Early Start constraint may also be assigned to a task with a Deadline Date.

❖ The Deadline Date may be displayed as a column and appears on the bar chart as a down arrow ⇩.

❖ An Indicator icon 🔯 is placed in the Indicator column when the Deadline Date creates Negative Float (Slack).

3.3 Negative and Free Float Bars

The **Gantt Chart Wizard**, available by clicking on the
🖳 icon or selecting **Format**, **Gantt Chart Wizard....**, is
a straightforward method of formatting your bars but
will not format and display the Negative Float and
Free Float bars. These will have to be added manually
using the **Bar Style** form by:

❖ **Format**, **Bar Styles...**, or double-click anywhere in
the Gantt Chart area except on an existing bar
(this will open the **Format Bar** form to format an
individual bar).

❖ Then add two bars as demonstrated below:

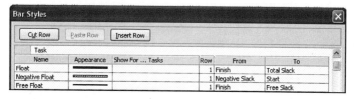

❖ **Negative Float** is generated when the Late Date is
calculated earlier than the Early Date and
represents the amount of time that the schedule
must catch up or how much earlier a project must
start to finish on time. Setting a Late constraint or
Deadline date earlier than the calculated Early
Date normally causes negative float.

❖ **Free Float** is the amount of time a task may be
delayed without delaying a successor task.

Note: Unlike some other some software, the Negative
Float is drawn from the Start Date of a task and not
the Finish Date. Therefore one bar is required for
Negative Float and one for Positive Float.

3.4   As Late As Possible Constraint

This constraint must be used with caution as it consumes Total Float (Slack) and therefore delays all successor activities does not just delay the task that the constraint is applied to.

❖ All Tasks in the picture below have Total Float:

❖ When Task C is made As Late As Possible then Task B develops Free Float:

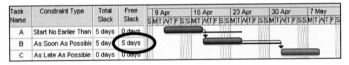

❖ When Task C is made As Soon As Possible and Task A is made As Late As Possible then Task A consumes all available Total Float and delays all the successors:

Some software packages offer a Zero Total Float function, which allow activities to be delayed and consume Free Float without delaying any successor activities. A Start to Finish relationship will drag a successor in front of it and act like a Zero Float constraint, but the use of this relationship is usually considered bad practice.

4 INTERESTING FEATURES

4.1 Wildcard Filters for Text Searching

The **Wildcard** functions are similar to the DOS Wildcard functions and are mainly used for filtering text:

❖ You may replace a single character with a "?". Thus, a filter searching for a word containing "b?t" will display words like "bat", "bit" and "but."

❖ You may replace a group of characters with an "*****". Thus, a filter searching for a word containing "b*t" will display "blot", "blight" and "but."

NOTE: For the Wildcard function to operate the "**equals**" Test must be used. This function does not work with the "**contains**" and in this mode "**equals**" works as a "**contains**" operand, see the picture below.

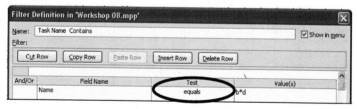

❖ **NA** allows the selection of a blank value. The filter below displays tasks without either a Baseline Start or Baseline Finish date:

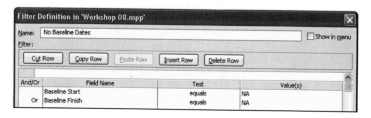

4.2   Interactive Filters

These filters allow you to enter the **Value(s)** of the filtered field after applying the filter. The filter is tailored each time it is applied via a user-prompt. The filter below will ask you to enter a word in the task name.

For this function to operate properly, the text in the **Value(s)** field must commence with a double quote and end with a double quote and question mark:

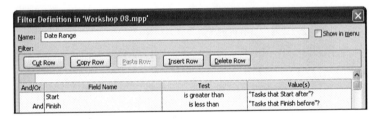

4.3   Selecting Dates

There is a slick way of selecting dates in date fields available in 2000 to 2003 but this function was eliminated in 2007:

Microsoft Project 2000–2003 has a function to enable the user to quickly scroll through days, months and years when editing dates from a column.

A calendar form is displayed by clicking on a date cell with the mouse pointer:

❖ To change the day, click on the required day.

❖ To change month either:

  ➢ Scroll a month at a time by clicking on the arrows on the top left-hand or top right-hand side of the form, or

  ➢ Click on the month at the top of the form and a drop-down list will be displayed to allow any month of the year to be selected.

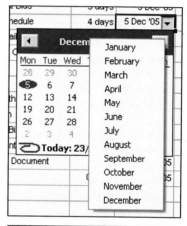

❖ To change the year, click on the year in the top of the form and scrolling arrows will be displayed allowing scrolling one year at a time.

When a date is selected from a column, Microsoft Project will set a constraint without informing the user. This may result in an incorrect constraint being set.

4.4 Understanding Start and Finish Milestones

❖ A Milestone is created by assigning a task duration of zero days.

❖ A Milestone is a Start Milestone when it has no predecessors.

❖ A Milestone is a Finish Milestone if it has one or more predecessors.

❖ A Start Milestone is at the Start of a Time Period, for example, 8:00 am.

❖ A Finish Milestone is at the End of a Time Period, for example, 5:00 pm.

	Task Name	Dur	Start	Finish	Predec-essors	2 April				
						M	T	W	T	F
1	Start MS	0d	Tue 8:00 AM	Tue 8:00 AM						
2	Task	2d	Tue 8:00 AM	Wed 5:00 PM	1					
3	Finish MS	0d	Wed 5:00 PM	Wed 5:00 PM	2					
4	Task	1d	Thu 8:00 AM	Thu 5:00 PM	3					
5	Finish MS	0d	Thu 5:00 PM	Thu 5:00 PM	4					

❖ A task may also be made to look like a task by checking the **Mark as a milestone** in the **Task Information** form **General** tab

❶	Duration	Start	Finish	14 May											21 May			
				T	F	S	S	M	T	W	T	F	S	S	M	T	W	T
1	6 days	7 May	14 May															
2	3 days	15 May	17 May										17/05					
3	4 days	18 May	23 May															

Note: Unlike some other scheduling software it is not possible for the user to assign a Milestone as either a Start or Finish Mile Stone in Microsoft Project.

4.5 Converting a Finish Milestone into a Start Milestone

Sometimes it is important to have a Start Milestone. For example, Task 5 in the picture below may be required on Friday morning not Thursday afternoon:

	Task Name	Dur	Start	Finish	Predec-essors	2 April M	T	W	T	F
1	Start MS	0d	Tue 8:00 AM	Tue 8:00 AM						
2	Task	2d	Tue 8:00 AM	Wed 5:00 PM	1					
3	Finish MS	0d	Wed 5:00 PM	Wed 5:00 PM	2					
4	Task	1d	Thu 8:00 AM	Thu 5:00 PM	3					
5	Finish MS	0mins	Thu 5:00 PM	Thu 5:00 PM	4					
6	Task	1d	Fri 8:00 AM	Fri 5:00 PM	5					

One workaround to achieve this:

❖ Add a duration, even if only 1 minute long, to the task that is to be the Start Milestone. The duration is not important.

❖ Check the **Mark as a Milestone** in the General tab of the Task Information form.

❖ Ensure all successors of the Start Milestone are Start to Start, otherwise all successors will span 1 day longer than their assigned duration:

➢ Without a Start to Start successor:

	Task Name	Dur	Start	Finish	Predec-essors		W	T	F	S	S	9 Apr M
4	Task	1d	Thu 8:00 AM	Thu 5:00 PM	3							
5	Finish MS	1min	Fri 8:00 AM	Fri 8:01 AM	4							
6	Task	1d	Fri 8:01 AM	Mon 8:01 AM	5							

➢ With a Start to Start successor:

	Task Name	Dur	Start	Finish	Predec-essors		W	T	F	S	S	9 Apr M
4	Task	1d	Thu 8:00 AM	Thu 5:00 PM	3							
5	Finish MS	1min	Fri 8:00 AM	Fri 8:01 AM	4							
6	Task	1d	Fri 8:00 AM	Fri 5:00 PM	5SS							

4.6 Elapsed Durations, Leads and Lags

4.6.1 Elapsed Durations

If you assign a task an **Elapsed** duration, the task will ignore all calendars and will be scheduled 24 hours a day and 7 days per week. To enter an elapsed duration, type an "**e**" between the duration and units.

❖ This is useful for tasks such as curing concrete or computer processes running 24 hours per day.

❖ The Total Float will calculate approximately three times longer than a task on an 8-hour per day calendar (depending on the length of the lunch break) and this may be misleading.

The example below shows the difference between a 7-**Elapsed Day** task and a 7-day task on a **Standard** (5-day per week) calendar.

Duration	Start	Finish		
7 edays	1 Sep 8:00 AM	8 Sep 8:00 AM		
7 days	1 Sep 8:00 AM	9 Sep 5:00 PM		

4.6.2 Float on Tasks with Elapsed Durations

The Float on Elapsed Duration tasks is calculated on a 24-hour per day calendar and will be different than a task on an 8-hour per day calendar:

	Duration	Total Slack		
1	12 days	0 days		
2	5 edays	10.38 edays		
3	5 days	7 days		

© Eastwood Harris

4.6.3 Elapsed Leads and Lags

An elapsed lead or lag may also be assigned to relationships and these also ignore all calendars:

Name	Duration	Successors	1 Sep							8 Sep					
			S	M	T	W	T	F	S	S	M	T	W	T	F	S
A	3 days	2FS+5 edays														
B	3 days	3FS-7 edays														
C	3 days															

4.7 Establishing Two Relationships between Two Tasks

Sometimes it is desirable to put two relationships between two activities, for example, a Start to Start and a Finish to Finish. It is not possible to put two relationships between two tasks in Microsoft Project unless a Milestone is inserted in the loop:

	Duration	Predecessors	Successors	16 Apr							23 Apr							30 Apr				
				S	M	T	W	T	F	S	S	M	T	W	T	F	S	S	M	T	W	T	F	S
1	10 days		3SS,2																				
2	0 days	1	3FF																				
3	5 days	1SS,2FF																					

	Duration	Predecessors	Successors	16 Apr							23 Apr							30 Apr				
				S	M	T	W	T	F	S	S	M	T	W	T	F	S	S	M	T	W	T	F	S
1	10 days		3SS,2																				
2	0 days	1	3FF																				
3	15 days	1SS,2FF																					

4.8   % Lags

A Percentage Lag increases the Lag duration as the predecessor duration increases:

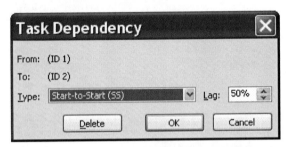

	Duration	Total Slack	Successors
1	5 days	0 days	2SS+50%
2	5 days	0 days	

	Duration	Total Slack	Successors
1	10 days	0 days	2SS+50%
2	5 days	0 days	

The lag duration is calculated on the successor calendar. When the successor task is changed from an 8-hour per day calendar to a 24-hour per day calendar, the elapsed duration of the successor is reduced, as well as the elapsed duration of the lag. Now the Float is calculated on a 24-hour per day basis. Things get a bit tricky here!

	Duration	Total Slack	Successor
1	5 days	0 days	2SS+50%
2	5 days	11.63 days	

Note: Microsoft Project 2000 calculates the lag on the Project Calendar.

4.9   Task Drivers

A **Driving Relationship** is the predecessor that determines the Early Start of a non-critical task that has two predecessors with have different finish dates. Microsoft Project 2000–2003 does not identify the difference between **Driving** and **Non-driving Relationships**, which often makes analyzing a schedule difficult. In these earlier versions of Microsoft Project, the simplest way to determine the driving relationship for tasks not on the critical path and with more than one predecessor was to delete the relationships until the task moved.

Microsoft Project 2007 introduced a **Task Drivers** form that indicates which is the driving predecessor and whether the schedule has been Resource Leveled. It also displays the effects of leveling.

Select the [Task Drivers] icon on the **Standard** toolbar to open the **Task Drivers** pane, which displays information as in the picture below:

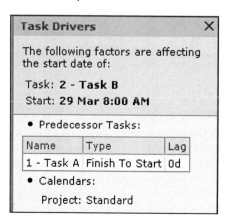

Task Drivers
The following factors are affecting the start date of:
Task: 2 - Task B
Start: 29 Mar 8:00 AM
• Predecessor Tasks:

Name	Type	Lag
1 - Task A	Finish To Start	0d

• Calendars:
    Project: Standard

4.10 Tracing the Logic

One method to trace the logic is to display the Bar Chart in the Top Pane and the Relationship Diagram in the Bottom Pane. Scroll up and down in the Gantt Chart to identify the predecessors and successors:

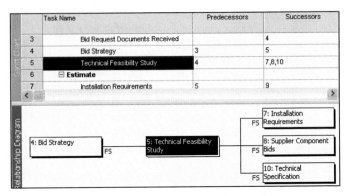

Another way is to display the Relationship Diagram in the Top Pane and the Task Form in the Bottom Pane. Click on the predecessors or successors in the Relationship Diagram to follow the logic:

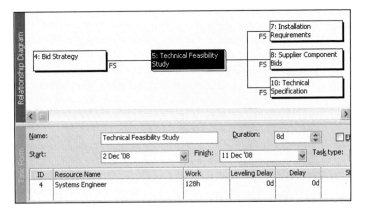

14570262202500006213673 2

Shell Fuel Vouchers ("Vouchers") are the property of Shell U.K. Oil Products Limited (as agent for Shell U.K. Limited), have no cash redemption value, are not for resale or publication and are valid at participating Shell Service Stations within GB only. Copied, damaged or defaced Vouchers will not be accepted. Vouchers can only be used once and only by the person to whom they are issued. Vouchers can be exchanged for the purchase of fuel only equivalent to their face value, or a higher value on payment of the difference. No change or credit note can be given for any excess. The maximum value of Vouchers that can be redeemed in a single transaction is £55. You must be 16 years or over to purchase petrol. This Voucher cannot be used in conjunction with any fuel payment card. This voucher expires on 31/11/2012. To the Retailer: For reimbursement, please return this Voucher to the clearing house no later than 28 days after expiry.

Issued by Shell U.K. Oil Products Ltd., Company No. 3625633, as agent for Shell U.K. Ltd., Company No. 140141, both with registered offices at Shell Centre, London SE1 7NA.

Shell

9 916538 850011

Your Shell Fuel Voucher

£2.50

Valid for any **Shell fuel**.

Voucher expires 30 November 2012.

Mr Ian Gladston
246122529

4.11 Creating a Hammock or LEO Task

A Hammock or Level Of Effort task is defined as a task that spans between two tasks or milestones and will change in duration when either of the driving dates change.

This is not a Summary Task created by Outlining and is not a Microsoft Project function but one may be created by:

❖ Assigning a Task Type that must not be **Fixed Duration** otherwise the duration will not change.

❖ A relationship is created between Start date of the driving Start milestone or task and Hammock Start date using the **Edit**, **Copy Cell...** and **Edit**, **Paste Special...**, **Paste Link...** link command.

❖ Then a relationship is created between finish date of the driving Finish milestone or task and Hammock Finish date using the **Edit**, **Copy Cell...** and **Edit**, **Paste Special...**, **Paste Link...** link command.

❖ As either of the Driving milestones or tasks is moved the Hammock will recalculate its duration.

❖ In the picture above there has bee a link created between the Start dates of task 2 and task 1 and the Finish dates of task 3 and task 1.

Note: A linked cell has triangle in the bottom right hand corner: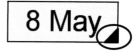

---

5 MAKING IT LOOK RIGHT

5.1 Date Format Dangers

There is often confusion on international projects between the numerical US date style (mmddyy) and the numerical European date style (ddmmyy). For example, in the United States 020710 is read as 07 Feb '10, and in many other countries as 02 Jul '10. Consider adopting the ddmmmyy style, **06 Jan '07** or mmmddyy style, **Jan 06 '07**.

Select **Tools**, **Options...** to display the **Options** form and select the **View** tab **Date format:**:

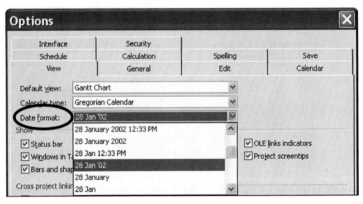

This option selects the display style of the dates for all projects. The date format options available will be dependent on your system default settings. You may adjust your system date format under the system Control Panel, Regional and Language Options.

5.2 Preventing the Date Format from Changing on Other Computers

The date format selected in the **Tools**, **Options...**, **View** tab applies to all projects opened on one computer. Some projects may require day and time and others day and month, so you have to keep changing the format each time you open a different project.

If you are in this situation, you may override the date format selected in the **Tools**, **Options...**, **View** tab by a date format selected in a **View**, **Table:**, **More Tables...** form:

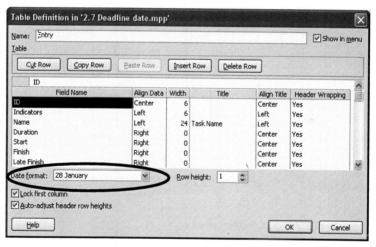

Each project could have its own set of tables all with their own project-specific date format.

When you send this project to someone else, they will have a better chance of seeing the same date format as you especially if their Start, Control Panel, Regional and Language Options are the same as yours.

5.3 *The Smart Way to Create Views*

A Single Gantt Chart View is made from a Gantt Screen and includes a Table, an optional Group and an optional Filter. A View also holds the Bar formatting and Print settings.

If your project will require multiple but similar Views, for example, headers and footers with the same print settings and bar formatting, the following process is recommended:

❖ Create the first View and get the Bar formatting and the Print settings right.

❖ The print preview Header, Footer and Legend should read all the text data from the **File**, **Properties** form so when a change in the text is required in all Views, it can be made in one place, the **File**, **Properties** form.

❖ Ensure that you have hidden all the bars that you do not want displayed in the Legend, by placing an "*****" in front of the bar name in the **Bars** form.

❖ Create new Views by copying the first View only after it has been checked, double-checked, and checked again.

❖ Each new View should have a unique name. This name is also used for the Table, Group and Filter names associated with the View, so each view has its own unique Table, Filter and Group.

❖ These uniquely named Tables, Groups and Filters should not be displayed in the menus to avoid their inadvertent application and corruption.

5.4   Bar Formatting

Select **Format, Layout...** to open the **Layout** form, which has some interesting features:

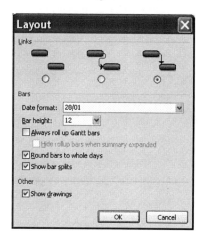

5.4.1   Bar Date Format

The Bar **Date format:** option sets the format for dates displayed on bars only.

The option to display dates on one or more selected bars is made using **Format, Bar...** or on all bars with **Format, Bar Styles...**.

5.4.2   Bar Heights

The **Bar height:** option sets the height of all the bars.

Individual bars may be assigned different heights by selecting a bar shape in the styles form.

5.4.3 Always Roll Up Gantt Bars

A̲lways roll up Gantt bars and **Hide rollup bars when summary expanded** works as follows:

❖ Tasks before roll up:

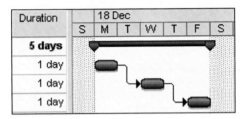

❖ Tasks with **A̲lways roll up Gantt bars** checked and **Hide rollup bars when summary expanded** unchecked, and both Summary and Detailed tasks displayed in the Bar Chart:

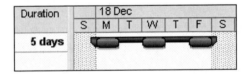

❖ Tasks with both **A̲lways roll up Gantt bars** and **Hide rollup bars when summary expanded** checked, the Summary Task bar is hidden when the Non Summary Tasks are rolled up:

❖ An individual bar may be rolled up to a summary task using the **Roll up Gantt bar to summary** option in the **Task Information** form when **Always roll up Gantt bars** options are unchecked.

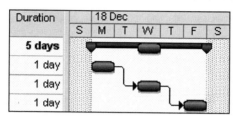

5.4.4 Round Bars to Whole Days

The **Round bars to whole days:** is used to make it easier to see short duration bars on a long duration schedule:

❖ When this option is unchecked, the length of the task will be shown in proportion to the total number of hours worked per day over the 24-hour time span. For example, an 8-hour working duration bar is shown below:

Duration			
	Tuesday	Wednesday	Thursday
1 day		▬	

❖ When this option is checked, the task bar is often displayed and spanned over the whole day irrespective of working time:

Duration			
	Tuesday	Wednesday	Thursday
1 day		▬▬▬	

5.4.5   Bar Text

Text may be placed on all bars using the **Format, Bar...** form or selected bars using the **Format, Bar Styles...** form.

Note: The length of the Bar Chart may be reduced by using a smaller font than the default or placing the text on top of the bar.

5.5   *Format Colors*

Colors are formatted in a number of forms and there is no single form for formatting all colors:

❖ **Nonworking time** colors in the Gantt Chart are formatted in the **Timescale** form; double-click on the timescale.

❖ **Text** colors are formatted in the **Text Styles** and **Font** forms, found under the **Format** command.

❖ **Gridline** colors are formatted in the **Gridlines** form, also found under the **Format** command.

❖ **Hyperlink** colors are formatted under **Tools, Options..., Edit** tab.

❖ **Timescale** and **Column Header** colors are formatted with the system color scheme used in the **Start, Settings, Control Panel, Display** option.

❖ The **Logic Lines**, also known as **Dependencies, Relationships,** or **Links,** inherit their color from the predecessor's bar color in the Gantt Chart view and may be formatted in the Network Diagram view by selecting **Format, Layout....**

5.6 Displaying an S-Curve

A single S-Curve may be created graphically and displayed by Microsoft Project by:

❖ Displaying the **Resource Sheet** in the top pane and selecting all the resources,

❖ Displaying the **Resource Graph** in the bottom pane,

❖ Right-clicking and displaying the **Cumulative Costs**, and

❖ Right-clicking, opening the **Bar Styles...** form and formatting as shown below:

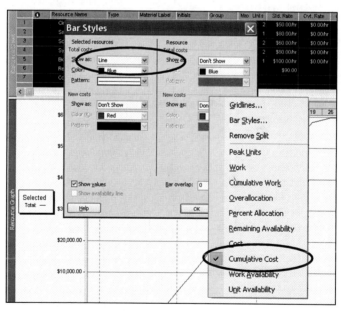

If more than one S-Curve is required then it is suggested that the data is exported to Excel using the **Analyze Timescale Data in Excel...** function from the **Analysis** toolbar.

5.7 Displaying Cumulative Histogram

This may be achieved in a similar way as an S-Curve by:

❖ Selecting **Cumulative Work** and

❖ Selecting the **Bar** option in the **Bar Styles...** form under **Total allocated work** for **Selected resources**.

5.8 Displaying a Project Summary Task

A Project Summary Task may be displayed by checking the **Show project summary task** box from the **Tools**, **Options...**, **View** tab.

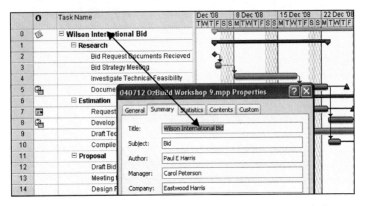

❖ This task spans from the first to the last task in the project and is, in effect, a built-in Level 1 outline.

❖ The description of the Summary Task is the Project Title entered in the **File**, **Properties** form.

❖ A Project Summary Task is a virtual task and may not have resources, relationships or constraints assigned.

5.9 Display Tasks without Successors as Critical

Normally a task that does not have successors will display Float, as per task 4 below:

	Total Slack	Critical	Successor	23 Apr	30 Apr	7 May
				S M T W T F S S	M T W T F S S	M T W T F S
1	0 days	Yes	2,4			
2	0 days	Yes	3			
3	0 days	Yes				
4	5 days	No				

❖ Select the **Tools**, **Options...**, **Calculation** tab,

❖ Check the **Calculate multiple critical paths** tab and then tasks:

> ➢ Without successors will have their Late Dates set to equal their Early Dates and will be calculated with zero Total Float (Slack),

> ➢ Displayed as critical in the bar chart and

> ➢ Are indicated critical in the Critical column.

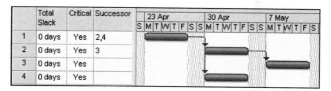

	Total Slack	Critical	Successor	23 Apr	30 Apr	7 May
				S M T W T F S S	M T W T F S S	M T W T F S
1	0 days	Yes	2,4			
2	0 days	Yes	3			
3	0 days	Yes				
4	0 days	Yes				

You might consider using this function when:

❖ You have not completed the schedule and want to show tasks without successors as critical, or

❖ You have few or no relationships in the schedule and you want to fool people into thinking that you have created a schedule where all tasks are on the critical path. In this situation, don't forget to hide the Indicators column!

5.10 *Preventing Descriptions from Indenting*

When a project has a number of Summary Task levels and the task descriptions are long then the Task Name column may have to be widened to display the full description:

	Task Name	Duration
1	⊟ **OzBuild Bid**	**38d**
2	⊟ **Research**	**9d**
3	Bid Request Documents Received	0d
4	Bid Strategy	1d
5	Technical Feasibility Study	8d
6	⊟ **Estimate**	**18d**

To prevent the Task Name from indenting select the **Tools**, **Options...**, **View** tab and uncheck the **Indent name** option:

	Task Name	Duration
1	⊟ **OzBuild Bid**	**38d**
2	⊟ **Research**	**9d**
3	Bid Request Documents Received	0d
4	Bid Strategy	1d
5	Technical Feasibility Study	8d
6	⊟ **Estimate**	**18d**

5.11 Reducing Column Widths

It is useful to reduce the width of columns so more data may be displayed on screen and in printouts. There are several ways to reduce column widths:

❖ To prevent the Task Name from indenting, select the **Tools**, **Options...**, **View** tab and uncheck the **Indent name** option.

❖ To reduce the width of the **Duration** column, select the **Tools**, **Options...**, **Edit** tab and under **View options for time units in 'Project 1':**

➢ **Minutes:, Hours:, Days:, Weeks:, Months:, Years:** – From the drop-down boxes, select your preferred designators for these units. Change "days" to "d" and "hr" to "h" to make the duration columns narrower.

➢ **Add space before label** – Places a space between the value and the label; uncheck this to make duration columns narrower.

➢ Change the column title from Duration to Dur:

❖ Change the date format to a shorter format in the **Tools**, **Options...**, **View** tab.

	Task Name	Duration	Start
1	⊟ **OzBuild Bid**	**38 days**	**1 December 2008**
2	⊟ **Research**	**9 days**	**1 December 2008**
3	Bid Request Documents Received	0 days	1 December 2008

	Task Name	Dur	Start
1	⊟ **OzBuild Bid**	**38d**	**1 Dec '08**
2	⊟ **Research**	**9d**	**1 Dec '08**
3	Bid Request Documents Received	0d	1 Dec '08

5.12 How to Display a Task ID that Will Not Change

One frustrating part of using Microsoft Project is that the Task ID is not unique and as new tasks are inserted then the ID changes. The Unique ID field helps resolve this issue, which is often very important in dispute resolution. Each task is assigned a Unique ID when it is created. This number is not used again in the schedule, even if the task is deleted.

There are two other columns that may be used to edit and display relationships using the Unique ID:

❖ The **Unique ID Predecessor**, and

❖ The **Unique ID Successor**.

The Task **Unique ID** allows users to identify easily which activities have been added or deleted or when a revised schedule has been submitted.

On the other hand, if one wants to reset the Unique ID, or hide the addition or deletion of tasks, then create a new schedule, transfer the calendars, etc. with **Organizer**, and copy and paste all the tasks into the new schedule.

There is also a unique **Resource ID** and a Resource Assignment **Unique ID**.

5.13 Hiding Task Information

Sometimes it is desirable to hide some information in a bar or cell about a specific task.

5.13.1 Hiding Bars

To hide a bar:

❖ Open **Task Information** from the **General** tab, and

❖ Check the **Hide task bar** option.

5.13.2 Hiding Text

To hide text in one or more cells:

❖ Select the cells,

❖ Select **Format**, **Font...** to open the **Font** form and make the Text color the same color as the Background, which is usually white.

5.14 Anchor a Vertical Line to a Milestone

It is often useful to have a vertical line on the Bar Chart to show the end of a Phase or Stage that will move as the project is rescheduled.

❖ Insert a vertical line on the Bar Chart using the **Insert**, **Drawing** function. Select the **Line** option and draw it on the screen.

❖ To attach the vertical line to a Task, double-click on the vertical line to open the **Format Drawing** form, select the **Size & Position** tab and select the Task ID to attach the line:

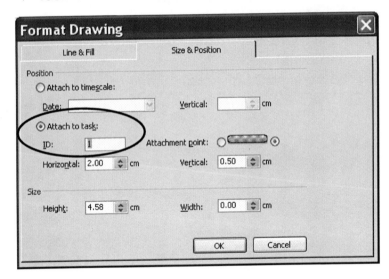

6 GETTING IT OUT - PRINTING

6.1 *Printing to One Page Wide*

Printing in Microsoft Project has always been a little problematic and requires a little patience to get right, but the following suggestions may assist:

❖ Create Views that are just used for printing and once they work do not edit them or use them for day-to-day maintenance of the schedule.

❖ If you wish to fit a schedule to one page wide it is usually best to make sure that most of the schedule fits onto the screen, or at least that the columns and bars each do not occupy more than 2/3 of the screen.

❖ Try printing to a pdf writer with an A3 or 11" x 17" paper size and then reduce the paper size when printing to an A4 or Letter paper size.

To reduce the width of columns, as discussed earlier:

❖ Select a narrow date format,

❖ Select the **Tools**, **Options...**, **Edit** tab and select a narrow format for the durations; for example, use "d" and not "days".

❖ Select the **Tools**, **Options...**, **Edit** tab and uncheck the **Add space before label option**. This will remove the space between the duration value and units.

❖ Consider increasing the row height so the Task Name column width may be reduced and text displayed on two or more lines.

6.2 Printing a Date Range

A date range may be selected from the Print form. In earlier versions of Microsoft Project, this had to be selected from the File menu, but in later versions these dates may be edited by selecting Print from the Print Preview form.

These dates are saved with the View so you may wish to consider creating a view for each date range.

In addition, a filter may be created to remove tasks that are not in the date range to be printed.

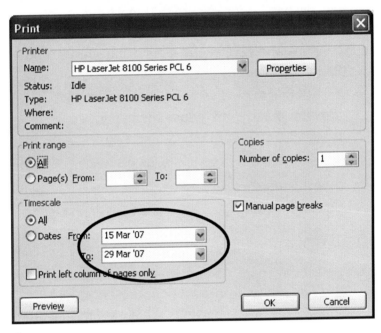

6.3 Printing a Gantt Chart and Resource Graph or Usage Table on One Page

Microsoft Project allows the display of a Gantt Chart in the Top Pane and a Resource Graph or Usage Table in the bottom pane but does not print the two panes in one printout in the way other software is able to do.

❖ One option is to print both reports to a pdf writer and then use the pdf software to create one file with both pages. The Gantt Chart and Table or Histogram will not be on the same page but will be one report. Programs like Adobe Acrobat enable this.

❖ Another is to use a screen capture program like SnagIt and copy both the top and bottom pane to Excel or Word to create a combined report.

6.4 Printing the Calendar

It is always useful to be able to print out the calendar for people to review the working hours and nonwork periods. The options are:

❖ Display and print the Calendar view, or

❖ Print a report using the **Report** (**Edit** in 2000–2003), **Reports...**, **Overview**, **Working Day** report.

It is useful to print the report to a pdf format so it may be saved, emailed and viewed by people who do not have Microsoft Project or do not know how to use it.

6.5 Hiding Some of the Bars in the Legend

When the Gantt Chart Wizard is used it creates a number of bars that are best not deleted as the use of certain functions such as Recurring Tasks rely on these formats to display the task bars.

To hide a bar type in the Legend, type an "*****" in front of the description in the **Bar Styles** form. This bar will still be displayed but will not be displayed in the Legend in Print Preview:

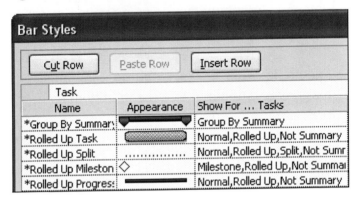

© *Eastwood Harris*

7 RESOURCE BASICS

7.1 How Many Resources Should I Have?

A resourced schedule may be created for the following purposes:

❖ **Estimating**. This type of schedule is used for estimating the cost and duration of a project or part of a project, such as a repeatable process. Many resources may be assigned to each task in an estimating schedule because it is not intended to status the schedule.

❖ **Control**. This type of schedule is used to monitor and control the progress of a project. In this situation the number of resources should be minimized as far as possible. This is because each resource assignment should be reviewed and possibly updated when the schedule is statused. Statusing a large schedule, with many tasks and many resources assigned to each task becomes a very time consuming operation. In this situation the scheduler may lose sight of their primary aim of forecasting the project end date, resource requirement and possibly the Final Forecast Cost. The schedule is now in danger of becoming an expensive time recording system and thus unable to provide essential forecast information. Thus the number of resources in a control schedule should be limited to the maximum number required to satisfy control and reporting requirements.

7.2 The Balance Between the Number of Activities and Resources

On large or complex schedules, you need to maintain a balance between the number of activities and the number of resources that are to be planned and tracked. As a general rule, the more activities a schedule has, the fewer resources should be created and assigned to tasks.

When a schedule has a large number of tasks and a large number of resources assigned to each task, the scheduler may end up in a situation where project team members are unable to understand the schedule and the scheduler is unable to maintain the schedule.

You may consider in this situation using resources that represent skills or trades instead of individual people, and on very large projects using crews or teams.

Updating a project with resources is substantially harder than without resources. The software is hard enough to maintain without adding the complexity of lots of resources that may not add value to the schedule.

It is critical to enter the minimum number of resources into a schedule as they consume a large amount of time to update.

7.3 Durations and Assignments Change as Resources are Assigned

Microsoft Project has some complex relationships that determine which parameters change when resources are added to tasks. These may result in durations or hours per resource reducing as resources are added to tasks.

This section will explain how resource assignments calculate and make some suggestions on how to set up the software so the tasks calculate the way you expect.

7.3.1 Task Type – Fixed Duration, Fixed Units, Fixed Work

Users must understand the relationship between the following parameters:

❖ The task **Duration**,

❖ The **Work** (the number of hours required to complete a task), and

❖ The **Units per Time Period** (the rate of doing the work or number of people working on the task).

The relationship is:

Duration x Units per Time Period = Work

For example, a 2-day task at 8 hours per day has a **Duration** of 2 x 8 =16 hours. If 2 people are assigned to the task the **Units per Time Period** is 2.00 or 200% and the work is 16 x 2 = 32 hours.

There are three options for the **Default task type:** which is assigned to a project in the **Tools, Options..., Schedule** tab. It may be changed for each task in the **Task Type** field that may be accessed in a number of places such as in a column and the **Task Information** form.

The **Default task type** decides how this relationship operates when one parameter changes. They are:

Fixed Duration	The **Duration** stays constant when either the **Units per Time Period** or **Work** are changed.
	A change to the **Duration** changes the **Work**.
Fixed Units	The **Units per Time Period** stay constant when either the **Duration** or **Work** is changed.
	A change to the **Units per Time Period** changes the **Duration**.
Fixed Work	The **Work** stays constant if either **Duration** or **Units per Time Period** are changed.
	A change to the **Work** changes the **Duration**.
	Therefore your estimate will not change when you change **Duration** or **Units per Time Period**.

7.3.2 Effort-Driven or Non Effort-driven?

The **Task Effort** is the combined number of hours of all work resources assigned to a task. The **Effort-driven** option determines how the effort is calculated as resources are added or removed from a **Fixed Units** or **Fixed Duration** task. There are two options:

Effort-driven	When a resource is added or removed from a task, the **Task Effort** assigned to a task remains constant. Adding or removing resources from a task will leave the total effort assigned to a task a constant unless all resources are removed or a change is made to the work of existing resource assignments.
Non Effort-driven	When a resource is added to or removed from a task, the **Resource Effort** or **Work** of other resources remains constant. Adding or deleting resources increases or decreases the total task effort and will not change the effort of assigned recourses.

In summary, as you assign resources:

❖ If you want the total number of hours assigned to stay constant then make the Task Effort-Driven.

❖ If you wish to assign each resource with its own hours or units per time period then make the task Non Effort-Driven.

Note: A **Fixed Work** task is automatically **Effort Driven**.

7.3.3   Task Type and Effort-Driven Options

If you are not sure which option to use then I recommend **Non Effort-driven** as a default. This option prevents changes to Task Durations and/or existing Resource assignments as Resources are added or removed from a task.

❖ Select **Fixed Units** for activities when the Units per time period must stay constant as either the Duration or Work is changed. For example, a crew of 1 Excavator and 3 Trucks must stay constant as the Duration or Work is changed.

❖ Select **Fixed Duration** for activities when the duration must not change as either resource Units per time period or Work is changed.

❖ Select **Fixed Work** if you wish the Work to stay constant as the duration is changed. The Task will be made **Effort-Driven** automatically with the **Effort-Driven** option grayed out. For example, a programmer assigned full-time for a week will have 40 hours' work. When the duration is doubled to a week, the programmer will work 50% of the time over 2 weeks but still work 40 hours. If you assign another person to help then the total Work will remain at 40 hours and the Duration not change.

The default for new Tasks is set in the **Tools**, **Options**…, **Schedule** tab. Click on the ⌈Set as Default⌋ icon and new projects will have these as their default options.

7.4   Assigning Resources to Tasks

There are many methods to assign resources to tasks. In summary, they are:

❖ Highlight one or more tasks that you want to assign resources. Click the **Assign Resources** icon 🗑 on the **Standard** toolbar to display the **Assign Resources** form.

❖ Open the bottom window displaying the **Task Detail Form**, **Task Form** or **Task Name Form**. Select the appropriate option from the **Format**, **Details** option or by right-clicking in the form.

❖ Double-click on a **Task** name or click on the **Task Information** icon 🗒 to open the **Task Information** form and select the **Resources** tab.

7.5   Resources and Summary Tasks

❖ Summary tasks may be assigned **Fixed Costs** and **Resources**.

❖ When a Work resource is assigned to a summary task the task type is set to **Fixed Duration** and **Non Effort- Driven**. This setting may not be changed. An increase in duration will increase Work.

❖ It is recommended that unless a Summary task Work resource assignment and costs are required to vary in proportion to the Summary task duration, then Work resources should not be assigned to a Summary task. You should consider using Fixed Costs, Cost resource or a Material resource if appropriate.

8 UPDATING ESSENTIALS

8.1 Baselines and Updating a Project

After a schedule has been reviewed and approved, it should be baselined. Setting the Baseline copies the **Early Start** and **Finish**, the **Original Duration** and each resource's **Costs** and **Work** into Baseline fields.

 Once the Baseline is set you will be able to update your plan and compare the progress with the original plan and be able to see:

❖ If the planned progress been achieved,

❖ Is the project ahead or behind schedule, and

❖ By how much in time and cost.

A Baseline is set by selecting **Tools**, **Tracking**, **Save Baseline….**

There are number of options and forms available to update the project after setting the Baseline. Irrespective of which forms are used there are two main methods to update a project:

❖ Auto Status the schedule by allowing the software to automatically update the tasks, as if the project progressed exactly according to schedule. Then, if required, adjust tasks to reflect actual events and revisions, or

❖ Update each task one by one.

8.2 Which Baseline Should Be Used?

After a project has progressed it may be necessary to set a new Baseline.

This may occur when the scope of a project has changed and a new baseline is required to measure progress against, but at the same time you may also want to keep a copy of the original baseline.

A new Baseline may be used to display the effect of scope changes on a plan by setting a Baseline, adding the scope change and comparing the revised schedule with the Baseline.

The **Baseline** data may be reviewed in some Views such as the **Task Details Form**, in columns and on the Bar Chart. You will be able to display the **Baseline 1** to **10** and **Interim Plan** dates and durations in columns and as a bar on the Gantt Chart but not in the forms. **Baseline 1** to **10** also do not have variance columns.

Therefore, it is recommended that the current baseline be saved as **Baseline** since the data is more accessible from the **Baseline** than **Baseline 1** to **10** and previous baselines should be copied to **Baselines 1** to **10**.

8.3 In-progress Task Finish Date Calculation

Many planning and scheduling packages calculate the Finish Date from the Data Date plus the Remaining Duration over the Task or Resource Calendar, whichever is applicable.

Unlike most planning and scheduling software packages, Microsoft Project ignores the Current Date and Status date when calculating an in-progress schedule. Instead it calculates the Finish date from the Actual Start Date plus the Duration and effectively ignores the Remaining Duration for normal calculation.

There is an in-built proportional link between **Duration**, **Actual Duration**, **Remaining Duration** and % **Complete**. It is not possible to unlink these fields (as in other scheduling software) and therefore not possible to enter the **Remaining Duration** independently of the % **Complete**.

Duration	% Comp.	Act. Dur.	Rem. Dur.	30 Apr								7 May					
				S	M	T	W	T	F	S	S	M	T	W	T	F	S
10d	0%	0d	10d														
10d	25%	2.5d	7.5d														
10d	100%	10d	0d														

Thus % **Complete** reflects the % of Duration of a task.

8.4 Current Date and Status Date

Microsoft Project has two project data date fields that may be displayed as vertical lines on the schedule. These dates may be edited from the **Project, Project Information...** form:

❖ **Current Date** – This date is set to the computer's date each time a project file is opened. It is used for calculating **Earned Value** data when a **Status Date** has not been set. The time of the **Current Date** is set by default to the start time of a day, see the picture below.

❖ **Status Date** – This field is blank by default with a value of **NA**. The Status Date will not change when the project is saved and reopened at a later date. It overrides the **Current Date** for calculating **Earned Value** data and is set by default to the finish time of a day, see the picture below.

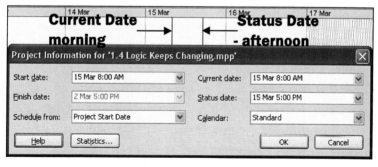

I recommend that the Status Date is set and displayed as a vertical line on a progressed schedule and the Current Date not displayed, because the Current Date represents the date today and does not normally represent any scheduling significance.

8.5 Auto Statusing Using Update Project

The Microsoft Project facility titled **Update Progress** is used for updating a project as if it had progressed according to plan. This function sets **Actual Start** and **Actual Finish** dates, **% Complete** and **Renaming Durations** in proportion to a user-assigned date, and also sets the **Status Date**.

Select **Tools**, **Tracking**, **Update Project...** to open the **Update Project** form:

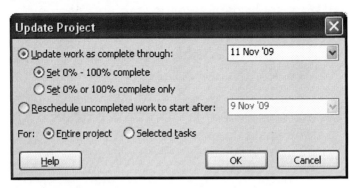

There are two options under **Update work as complete through:** which apply to in-progress tasks only.

❖ **Set 0% – 100 % complete** and this is the recommended option which sets the progress in line with the **Status Date**, or

❖ **Set 0% or 100 % complete only**. This option leaves the % Complete at zero until the task is 100% complete. Tasks often look behind schedule, but this option supports the progress measurement philosophy of not awarding progress until the task is complete.

8.6 Moving Incomplete Work into the Future by Splitting

There is a feature which will schedule the **Incomplete Work** of an **In-Progress** task to start on a specific date in the future:

❖ If you want to apply this operation to some tasks, then these should be selected first.

❖ Select the **Tools**, **Options...**, **Schedule** tab and ensure the **Split in-progress tasks** option is checked otherwise this function will not operate.

❖ Select **Tools**, **Tracking**, **Update Project...** to open the **Update Project** form:

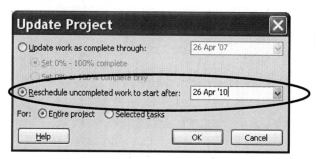

❖ Click on the **Reschedule uncompleted work to start after:** radio button.

❖ Specify the date after which incomplete work should commence in the drop-down box to the right and click on the OK button.

Note: This function does not set the **Status Date** and may be different to the **Status Date**. It is therefore effectively another **Data Date**.

8.7 Tracking Toolbar

The tracking toolbar may be displayed by selecting **View**, **Toolbars** and selecting the **Tracking** toolbar.

❖ Displays the **Project Statistics** form.

❖ **Update as Scheduled** updates the selected task as if it has proceeded exactly as it was scheduled. An in-progress or completed task could be dragged to where it actually happened and then the button clicked to progress the task.

❖ **Reschedule Work** will split a task that is behind schedule and place the incomplete portion after the Status Date. For this function to work the check the **Split in Progress task** box in the **Tools**, **Options...**, **Schedule** tab must be checked.

❖ **Add Progress Line** will add a progress line that shows if tasks are ahead or behind schedule. **Tools**, **Tracking**, **Progress Lines...** opens the **Progress Lines** form where the lines are formatted. A Baseline should be set to provide a comparison to the original plan. Multiple Progress lines may be recorded.

❖ **Percent Complete** buttons set the percent complete as indicated by the button and may be used in conjunction with the Reschedule Work button.

❖ **Update Tasks** opens the **Update** Tasks form.

8.8 Why Do Calculation Options – Move end of completed parts...Not Work?

These new functions were introduced in Microsoft Project 2002 intended to assist schedulers to place the new tasks as they are added to the schedule in a logical position with respect to the **Status Date**. This function is difficult to use and some practice is required to make it work properly. Here are some tips if you are unable to get it to work:

❖ Select the **Tools**, **Options...**, **Calculation** tab and these options are found under the **Calculation options for 'Project Name'**:

❖ If the **Status Date** has not been set then the **Current Date** is used.

For all these options to operate all four of the following parameters must be met:

❖ The **Split in-progress tasks** option in the **Schedule** tab must be checked, and

❖ The required option on the **Calculation** tab must be checked before the task is added or edited, and

❖ The **Updating task status updates resource status** option on the **Calculation** tab must be checked, and

❖ The Task **MUST NOT BE** assigned **Task Duration Type** of **Fixed Duration**.

❖ These options may NOT be turned on and off to recalculate all tasks. The options only work on new tasks when they are added to a schedule or when a task is updated by changing the % Complete.

❖ This function will ignore constraints even when the Schedule Option **Tasks will always honor their constraint dates** has been set.

❖ This function may not be applied to existing schedules, but only to new tasks if the options are set before the tasks are added or when a task % Complete is updated.

This function in its current form has some restrictions that schedulers may find unacceptable:

❖ Existing schedules may not be opened and the function applied.

❖ When the **Move start of remaining parts before status date forward to status date** is used, it will change any **Actual Start** date that you have entered prior to entering a % Complete. Changing an Actual Date is not a desirable event.

This option should be used with caution and users should ensure they fully understand how this function operates by statusing a simple practice schedule multiple times.

8.9 Comparing Progress with Baseline

There will normally be changes to the schedule dates and more often than not these are delays. The full extent of the changes is not apparent without a Baseline bar to compare with the statused schedule.

❖ To display the **Baseline Bar** in the **Bar Chart** you may use either the **Format, Bar Styles...** function, or

❖ You may use the **Gantt Chart Wizard** as follows:

➢ Select **Format, Gantt Chart Wizard...** to open the Gantt Chart Wizard.

➢ Select the **Baseline** or **Custom Gantt Chart** option to format the Gantt Chart to display both the current schedule and the baseline.

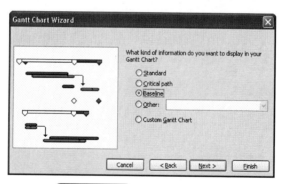

➢ Hit the [Next >] button and follow the remainder of the instructions to complete the formatting. You will be given options for applying text and relationships in the Gantt Chart.

This wizard will overwrite any customized formatting you have made using the **Format, Bar Styles...** option.

The Start and Finish Date variances are available by displaying the **Start Variance** and **Finish Variance** columns. These variance columns use the **Baseline** data and variance columns and are not available for **Baseline 1** to **10**. Therefore, the current Baseline should be established as Baseline and older Baselines copied to Baseline 1 to 10.

Start 1 to 10 and Finish1 to 10 may also be used as interim Baselines of un-resourced schedules.

8.10 Progress Lines

Some users like to display **Progress Lines**, which are usually shown as zigzag lines on the Gantt Chart showing how far ahead or behind the project tasks are.

Select **Tools**, **Tracking**, **Progress Lines...** to open the **Progress line** form where the progress lines may be formatted:

	Task Name	Finish Variance	W	T	F	S	S
6	⊟ **Estimate**	**0d**					
7	Installation Requirements	-1d					
8	Supplier Component Bids	0d					
9	Project Schedule	-1d					
10	Technical Specification	-3d					

8.11 Simple Procedure for Statusing a Schedule – Using Auto Status

For those people who require just one simple method of statusing a schedule the following process should be considered, but may not suit all situations especially when a project is way off plan:

❖ Set the Baseline by selecting **Tools, Tracking, Save Baseline....**

❖ Display the Baseline bars by selecting **Format, Gantt Chart Wizard....**

❖ Display the Status Date Gridline, select **Format, Gridlines...**, select **Status Date**.

❖ Select **Tools, Tracking, Update Project...** to open the **Update Project** form and select **Set 0% – 100 % Complete**, set the date in the form to the new **Status Date**.

❖ The project should be statused as if it has progressed exactly as planned and the Status Date should now be displayed in the bar chart.

❖ Displaying the **Tracking Table** may assist here.

❖ Now adjust the task dates by dragging the bars or entering the dates in the appropriate column; the order that the actions take place is important:

➢ **Complete tasks** should have the Actual Start and then the Actual Finish dates adjusted, in this order, to the date that the task actually started and actually finished. If you adjust the Finish date first then the Start date, you will then have to readjust the Finish date again.

> ➤ **Completed Milestones** will be changed to a Task if an Actual Finish date is entered, so only enter an Actual Start and 100% if a Milestone is complete.

> ➤ **In-Progress tasks** should have the Actual Start entered first, then the task bar dragged or Duration adjusted so the finish date is where it is expected to finish, and finally the % Complete adjusted.

> ➤ **Unstarted tasks** should have their logic and durations revised.

> ➤ Consider using the **Tracking** toolbar at this point.

❖ Add any scope changes to the schedule.

❖ Save the project with a new filename and save for future reference.

8.12 Procedure for Detailed Statusing

This procedure is suited to people who wish to update a schedule properly and make sure the Actual dates and Remaining Durations of Tasks are correct. It has small but important differences to the previous process:

❖ Ensure that everyone on the project team is aware of the reporting cycle, the updating procedure and review process.

❖ Set the Baseline by selecting **Tools**, **Tracking**, **Save Baseline...**.

❖ Display the Baseline bars by selecting **Format**, **Gantt Chart Wizard...**.

❖ Select the **Gantt Chart** view and you may find the Tracking Table useful to apply.

❖ Display the Variance columns as required; the **Finish Variance** is always a popular column to display.

❖ Display the Status Date Gridline and hide the current date by selecting **Format**, **Gridlines**...; select **Status Date**.

❖ Display the **Tracking** toolbar by selecting **View**, **Toolbars**.

❖ Now enter the task status for each task one at a time by entering the information in the appropriate column.

❖ The order in which the actions take place is important:

> ➢ **Complete tasks** should have the Actual Start and then the Actual Finish dates adjusted, in this order, to the date that the task actually started and actually finished. If you adjust the Finish date first, then the Start date, you will have to readjust the Finish date again.

> ➢ **Completed Milestones** will be changed to a Task if an Actual Finish date is entered, so only enter an Actual Start and 100% if a Milestone is complete,

> ➢ **In-Progress tasks** should have the Actual Start entered first, then the task bar dragged or Duration adjusted so the finish date is where it is estimated to finish and finally the % Complete adjusted.

> ➢ Tasks that are behind schedule may be split with the ⊞ **Reschedule Work** icon on the **Tracking** toolbar. Make sure that the **Tools, Options...**, **Schedule** tab, **Split in-progress tasks** box is checked:

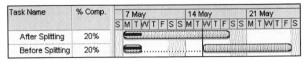

> ➢ **Unstarted tasks** should have their logic and durations revised.

❖ Add any scope changes to the schedule.

❖ Save the project for future reference with a new filename.

8.13 *Preparing to Update with Resources*

Statusing Microsoft Project schedules with resources:

❖ Uses a number of features that are very interactive and difficult to comprehend,

❖ Requires experience in the software,

❖ Needs significant time to complete the process, and

❖ As a result it is often difficult to achieve the desired result.

I suggest that before you work on a live project that you:

❖ Create a simple schedule with a couple of tasks and assign two or three resources against each task.

❖ Set the **Options** to reflect the way you want to enter the information and how you want Microsoft Project to calculate.

❖ Go through the statusing process with dummy data and then check that the results are as you expected.

You will need to consider how the measure of progress at the summary task level will be displayed:

❖ The **% Complete** is the % of Duration and the **Summary Task % Complete** is based on the proportion of all the Actual Durations divided by the sum of all the Durations. The summary % Complete may often be very misleading. The picture below shows the project is 20% through the duration but the % Complete shows 60%:

	Task Name	% Comp.	May					Jun	
			30	7	14	21	28	4	11
1	⊟ **Summary**	**60%**							
2	Task 1	100%							
3	Task 2	100%							
4	Task 3	100%							
5	Task 4	100%							
6	Task 5	100%							
7	Task 6	20%							

❖ The **% Work** field is calculated from the proportion of the **Actual Work** to **Work** and is summarized at summary task correctly:

	Task Name	% Comp.	% Work Complete	Work	Act. Work	) Apr	7 May	14 May	21 May
						T WT F S S MT WT F S S MT WT F S S MT WT			
1	⊟ **Summary**	**47%**	**71%**	**240 hrs**	**170 hrs**				
2	Task 1	100%	100%	120 hrs	120 hrs	Resource[3]			
3	Task 2	40%	63%	80 hrs	50 hrs		Resource[2]		
4	Task 3	0%	0%	40 hrs	0 hrs				Resource

❖ The **% Work** and **% Complete** fields may be unlinked with the **Tools**, **Options...**, **Calculation** tab **Updating task status updates resource status:** option. If unlinked, the **% Work** may be different from **% Complete**. See the picture above.

Other points to consider are:

❖ Do you wish Microsoft Project to calculate the resource **Actual Costs** with the option **Actual costs are always calculated by Microsoft Project** checked?

❖ Do you wish your incomplete tasks to be split and scheduled to start after a date using the **Reschedule uncompleted tasks to start after:** in conjunction with the **Split** task option?

8.14 Updating Resources

There are a number of places that resources may be updated:

❖ The **Task Details** form, **Task Information** form, **Task** form, **Resource** form, **Resource Name** form may be used to enter the quantities and costs to date and quantities to complete. Using this method it is simple to end up with actual work and costs in the future or remaining work and cost in the past, which is illogical and should be avoided.

❖ The **Task Usage View** and **Resource Usage View** may be used to enter the data per day or week depending on the timescale. This method takes more effort but will ensure Actuals are in the past and Remaining Work and Costs are in the future.

A couple of other points:

❖ **Fixed Costs** update automatically in proportion to the % Complete. **Cost Resources** are available in Microsoft Project 2007, which does not have a Quantity, allows a little more flexibility than Fixed Costs.

❖ When **Actual costs are always calculated by Microsoft Project**? is unchecked Actual Costs are NOT calculated and you will need to enter your own.

❖ Cost to Complete are always calculated by Microsoft Project from the resource Rates.

❖ If you assign Overtime to a resource make sure you have an Overtime rate; otherwise, as you assign Overtime the Forecast Cost will reduce.

9 OTHER THINGS OF INTEREST

9.1 Standardizing Projects

It is often important to be able to create schedules that have standard characteristics such as calendars tailored with your local or organization's holidays, or layouts and filters to present schedules in a standard format. There are several methods of standardizing new projects:

❖ **Global .mpt** which is used to create new projects when the **File**, **New**, **Blank Project** command is used, and

❖ Creating and saving **Templates**.

❖ Creating a "Standard Project" and copying it.

9.2 Global.mpt

The **Global.mpt** may not be opened with Microsoft Project and is part of the Microsoft Project Installation on each computer. This function may be used to standardize projects if you are the only person creating new projects.

❖ A new blank project copies default values such as the Standard Calendar from the **Global.mpt** file.

❖ The **Global.mpt** file may be edited using the **Tools**, **Organizer...** utility. The source project has to be open to copy data into the Global.mpt.

9.3 *Templates*

A template is a complete project that is saved and then copied in the process of creating a new project.

❖ ***.mpt** file format is used for saving Microsoft Project templates.

❖ Select **File**, **New** to open the start-up **Task Pane**. There are several options for template locations:

> ➤ **Templates on Office Online**, this will take you to a Microsoft web page through Microsoft Explorer.

> ➤ **On my computer...**, this will allow you to open templates on your computer.

> ➤ **On my Web sites...**, this opens an Explorer-style window where web site addresses may be recorded.

❖ Templates accessed **On my computer...**are saved and accessed from the **User templates** directory that is specified in the **Tools**, **Options...**, **Save** tab.

❖ Organizational templates may be accessed by:

> ➤ Allowing people to copy the organizational templates from a corporate location, or receive them by email, and save them on the local drive. This process is suitable when the users do not always have a network connection.

> ➤ Mapping the **User templates** directory to a location on a corporate network drive.

9.4 Copying Views, Tables and Filters

The **Global.mpt** file holds the schedule's default settings such as **Tables** and **Views**, which are inherited by new projects that are not created from a template.

The **Organizer** function is used to copy information between projects or to update the **Global.mpt**.

❖ Select **Tools**, **Organizer...**to open the **Organizer** form:.

❖ The projects you want to copy settings to and from will have to be opened in order to copy data from one schedule to another, except for the **Global.mpt** project.

❖ The Organizer function is used for renaming and deleting most items such as **Tables**, **Views and Calendars**.

❖ The two tabs with titles that are not self-explanatory are:

➢ **Maps** – These are predefined tables for exporting data, and

➢ **Modules** – These are Visual Basic Macros.

9.5 Editing Tool Bar Icons

To edit the Tool bar icons

❖ **Right-Click** in the toolbar area,

❖ Select **Customize...**,

❖ Select the **Commands** tab,

❖ Drag icons onto the required tool bar, or

❖ Drag icons off the toolbar to remove them.

99 TRICKS & TRAPS for Microsoft Office Project

9.6 Right-Clicking with the Mouse

It is very important that you experiment with the right mouse button as every part of the Microsoft Project screen has a different menu.

9.7 Always Displaying Full Menus

It is often annoying to wait for the full menus to be displayed, especially as the ones you normally want to use are hidden.

To ensure the full menus are always displayed:

❖ **Right-Click** in the toolbar area,

❖ Select **Customize...**,

❖ Select the **Options** tab,

❖ Check **Always show full menus**:

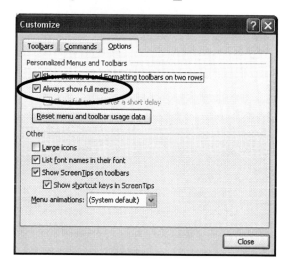

9.8 Dynamically Linking Cells

It is also possible to dynamically link data to other programs such as an Excel spreadsheet:

❖ Copy the data from the spreadsheet,

❖ Select the cell position in the table where the data is to be pasted in Microsoft Project,

❖ Select **Edit**, **Paste Special** and then select the **Paste Link** and **Text Data** options,

❖ The data will be pasted into the cell(s) and changes to linked cells in the spreadsheet or other program will be reflected in the Microsoft Project schedule.

❖ The linked cell will have a little triangle in the bottom right-hand side.

❖ Be careful when linking dates fields as this sets constraints.

❖ When you reopen the project schedule at a later date you will be asked if you wish to refresh the data from the other application.

❖ Delete or change the cell data to remove a link.

❖ Double-click on the little triangle in the cell to open the link.

❖ It is also possible to link one or more cells in a schedule with another cell in the same schedule so a change in one cell will change all the other linked cell(s). Use the **Paste Link** option.

9.9 How Does Negative Float Calculate for Summary Activities?

The lowest value of the Total Float of incomplete tasks is adopted by the summary task:

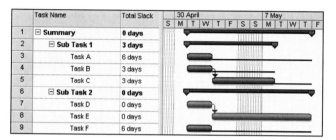

In the picture below, Task C is the latest task and has Float, but Sub Task 1 has adopted zero float from Task D the lowest float value.

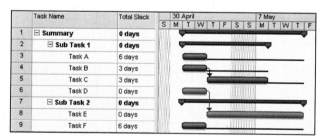

Now the project has progressed and the task with zero float is complete. Sub Task 1 has 3 days' Float.

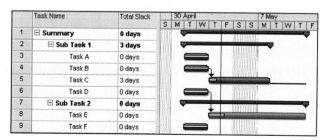

9.10 *Float and Constraints*

The following principles apply to constraints:

❖ **Early** constraints operate on **Early dates,**

❖ **Late** constraints operate on **Late dates,**

❖ **Start** constraints operate on **Start dates,** and

❖ **Finish** constraints operate on **Finish dates.**

The picture below demonstrates how constraints calculate Total Float (Slack) of tasks (without predecessors or successors) against the first task of 10 days' duration.

Tasks 9 and 10 have a Deadline Date assigned which allows a second constraint to be applied to a task and operates like a Finish No Later Than constraint.

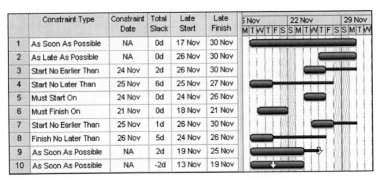

	Constraint Type	Constraint Date	Total Slack	Late Start	Late Finish	
1	As Soon As Possible	NA	0d	17 Nov	30 Nov	
2	As Late As Possible	NA	0d	26 Nov	30 Nov	
3	Start No Earlier Than	24 Nov	2d	26 Nov	30 Nov	
4	Start No Later Than	25 Nov	6d	25 Nov	27 Nov	
5	Must Start On	24 Nov	0d	24 Nov	26 Nov	
6	Must Finish On	21 Nov	0d	18 Nov	21 Nov	
7	Start No Earlier Than	25 Nov	1d	26 Nov	30 Nov	
8	Finish No Later Than	26 Nov	5d	24 Nov	26 Nov	
9	As Soon As Possible	NA	2d	19 Nov	25 Nov	
10	As Soon As Possible	NA	-2d	13 Nov	19 Nov	

The **Late** constraints reduce the amount of float a task has and may generate **Negative Float**.

The **Must** constraints act like an Early and Late constraint in one.

9.11 Using Custom Fields

Select **Tools**, **Customize Fields...** to open the **Customize Fields** form. This function includes a number of predefined fields for both Task and Resources.

❖ Task fields may be used for recording additional information about Tasks (such as responsibility, location, floor, system) and may be displayed in Task Views such as the Gantt Chart.

❖ Resource fields may record information such as telephone number, address, office and skills and may be displayed in Resource Views such as the Resource Sheet.

❖ The fields may be **Renamed**. For example, the Task Text 1 field may be renamed "Responsibility" and the name of the person responsible for the task (this may not be the resource assigned to the task) placed in the Responsibility (Text 1) column.

❖ A renamed field is then available in the Task Information or Resource Information Custom Fields tab.

❖ Formulas may be created to populate the task fields with calculated data.

❖ Tasks and Resources may be Grouped using Custom Fields.

These predefined fields fall into the following categories: Cost, Date, Duration, Finish (date), Flag, Number, Outline Code (this option is on a separate Tab in Microsoft Project 2000–2003), Start (date) and Text.

9.12 *Custom Columns Formulas and Drop-Down List*

The **Custom Attributes** section of the **Custom Fields...** form is used to define Lookup lists and Formulas

❖ **None** allows data to be entered into the field without any restrictions from either a column or an Information form.

❖ Lookup... opens the **Edit Lookup Table** where a table of values and descriptions may be entered. The Value is displayed in columns and Description in bands when the tasks are grouped by this field.

❖ Formula... allows the assigning of formulas for the calculation of field values from other task and project fields.

The **Calculation for task and group summary rows** specifies how summary tasks calculate their values, such as Maximum, Minimum, Sum, None and Average:

❖ Dates could be Minimum or Maximum, and

❖ Cost would use Sum.

Calculation for assignment rows determines if the field value is displayed against the resource or the resource and assignment in Task Usage and Resource Usage fields in Microsoft Project 2007.

Value to display allows the options of displaying the value in the cell or generating graphical indicators such as traffic lights.

© *Eastwood Harris*

9.13 *Custom Outline Codes*

There are ten hierarchical Task Custom Outline Codes and ten hierarchical Resource Outline Codes that may be renamed to suit the project requirements.

❖ Task Custom Outline Codes may be used for any hierarchical project breakdown structure, such as a PRINCE2 Product Breakdown Structure, Contract Breakdown Structure, Work Breakdown Structure and

❖ Resource Custom Outline Codes may be used for organizational breakdown structures such as the hierarchy of authority, locations and departments.

The 2007 forms are slightly different from the 2000–2003 forms. The process to use this function has the following steps:

❖ Define the new Outline Code structure,

❖ Assign the codes to the tasks or resources, and

❖ Create a Group to organize the tasks under the new Custom Outline Code structure.

9.13.1 Define a Custom Outline Code Structure

Select **Tools, Customize, Fields...** to open the form:

❖ An Outline Code may be created for either **Task** or **Resource** data by clicking on the appropriate radio button under the title **Field**.

❖ Select the Outline Code tab in 2000–2003 or select Outline Code from the drop-down box in 2007.

❖ The [Import Field...] function allows you to copy a code structure from another project in a method similar to Organizer.

❖ The [Rename...] button opens a form to edit the name of the Outline Code.

❖ The [Lookup...] button in Microsoft Project 2007 opens the **Edit Look Up Table** form for the selected Outline Code to create the **Lookup table**.

❖ Define the **Mask** or code structure by clicking on the [Edit Mask...] button at the top right-hand side in 2007, or clicking the [Define Code Mask...] button in 2000–2003 before entering the codes. This will open the **Outline Code Definition** form where the code structure is defined:

  ➢ As each **Level** is created it is assigned a number.

  ➢ The **Sequence** defines the type of text that may be entered for the code: Numbers, Upper Case, Lower Case or Characters (text).

  ➢ The **Length** specifies how many characters the Code Level may have: any, or a number between 1 and 10.

  ➢ The **Separator** defines the character that separates each level in the structure.

❖ The picture displays 4 levels each using a different option for their code:

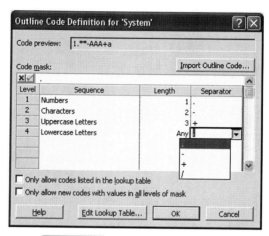

❖ Click the [OK] button to return to the **Edit Lookup Table** form where the Code Values and Descriptions are entered. The picture shows two levels for a Power Station Unit and Equipment:

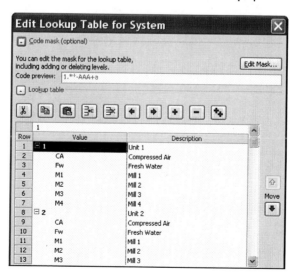

9.13.2 Assigning the Custom Codes

The codes are assigned by:

❖ Displaying the appropriate column:

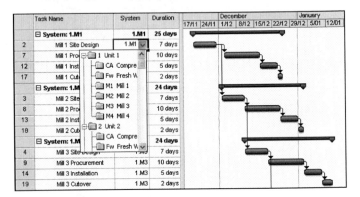

❖ Or by opening the Task Information or Resource
Information form:

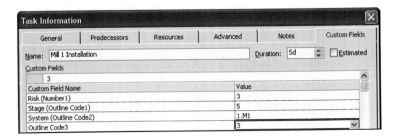

9.13.3 Grouping with Custom Data

Grouping allows grouping of tasks under data items such as Customized fields, Durations, Constraints, etc. This function is useful to group related tasks that are spread throughout a project schedule.

The Grouping function works in a similar way to Filters and Tables. A predefined Group may be assigned by:

❖ Selecting **Project**, **Group by**:

❖ Then either:

> ➢ Selecting a group from the list, or

> ➢ Selecting **More Groups...** to open the **More Groups** form, clicking on the **Task** or **Resource** radio button, and then selecting one from the list.

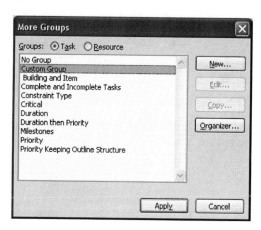

To create a new Group:

❖ Select **Project**, **Group by:**, **More Groups...** to open the **More Groups** form,

❖ Click on the [New...] button to open the **Group Definition** form,

❖ Now create a "Grouping" which may be reapplied at a later date or copy to another project using **Organizer**.

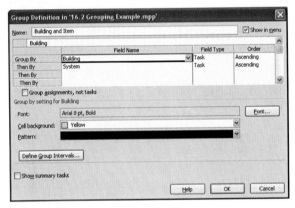

❖ The **Define Group Interval** form is available with many **Group By** options, such as Start or Finish, and allows further formatting options by defining the intervals of the banding.

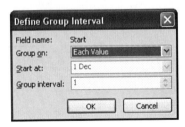

The picture below shows a project Grouped by 2 text fields that have been renamed Systems and Building. Note the order of the Task Numbers:

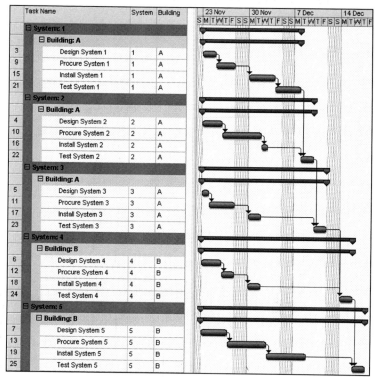

9.14 Exporting to Excel

The **Analysis** toolbar is designed to export time-phased data to Excel where charts may be created. This is a wizard-style function and the instructions will take you through the process, which results in tabular format of the data in Excel.

Data may be saved to and imported from Excel files using **File/Save**, **File/Save As** and **File/Open**.

9.15 Turning Off Getting Started and Project Guide

These guides often slow down experienced users as they have to be continually closed:

❖ To prevent the pane titled **Getting Started** from appearing every time Microsoft Project is opened, select **Tools**, **Options...**, select the **General** tab and uncheck the **Show Startup Task pane** box.

❖ To prevent the **Project Guide** pane from appearing every time Microsoft Project is opened, select **Tools**, **Options...**, select the **Interface** tab and uncheck the **Display Project Guide** box.

9.16 Contingent Time

It is important that this subject is considered and may be included using a number of techniques:

❖ Adding one or more tasks, that may be reduced in duration as contingent time is consumed to keep the project end date constant.

❖ Increasing all task durations by a factor.

❖ Making some calendar work days as non work.

9.17 Do I Have All the Scope?

Many schedules are unrealistic or do not calculate a realistic Critical Path because the whole scope has not been entered into a schedule. There are a couple of techniques that may be employed to ensure the whole scope has been included:

❖ Stakeholder Analysis, and

❖ Risk Analysis.

9.17.1 Stakeholder Analysis

Many project managers conduct a **Stakeholder Analysis** at the start of a project. This process identifies all the people and organizations with an interest in the project and their interests.

❖ You may use a stakeholder analysis to identify all the stakeholders and their activities. The findings must be included in the schedule.

❖ Key project success factors may be identified from the interests of the most influential stakeholders.

❖ The stakeholder analysis may be used as the basis of a communications plan.

9.17.2 Risk Analysis

❖ The process of planning a project may identify risks and a formal risk analysis should be considered. A risk analysis may identify risk mitigation activities that should be added to the schedule before it is submitted for approval.

© Eastwood Harris

9.18 Preparing for Dispute Resolution

Dispute resolution is becoming more frequent. There are some steps that may be taken to prepare for this eventuality which should reduce the cost of this process.

9.18.1 Keeping Electronic Copies of Each Update

Each time you report to the client or management, it is recommended that you save a copy of your project and change the file name (perhaps by appending a date to the file name or using a revision or version number) or create a subdirectory for each version of the project. This allows you to reproduce these reports at any time in the future and an electronic copy will be available for dispute resolution purposes.

9.18.2 Clearly Record the Effect of Each Change

Each change should be clearly recorded. Consider if you should:

- ❖ Create a copy of the schedule for each scope change analysis,
- ❖ Set the Baseline before entering the scope change,
- ❖ Add new tasks for scope changes and do not extend existing tasks,
- ❖ Show delays as tasks, not lags or constraints,
- ❖ Ensure the elapsed duration of the delay is calculated.

INDEX